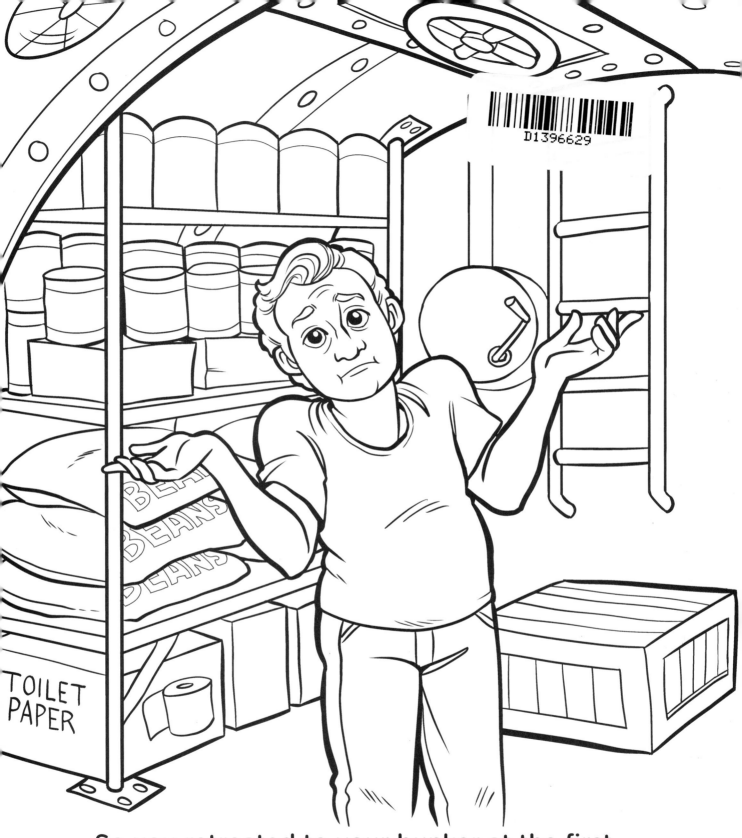

So you retreated to your bunker at the first
sign of the end of the world. What next?

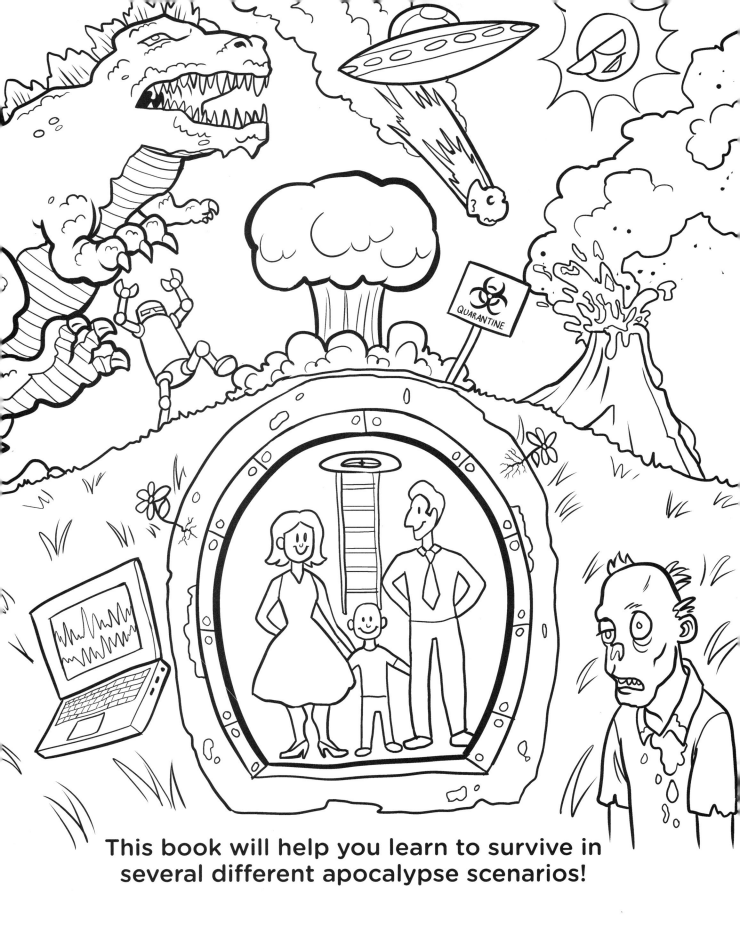

This book will help you learn to survive in several different apocalypse scenarios!

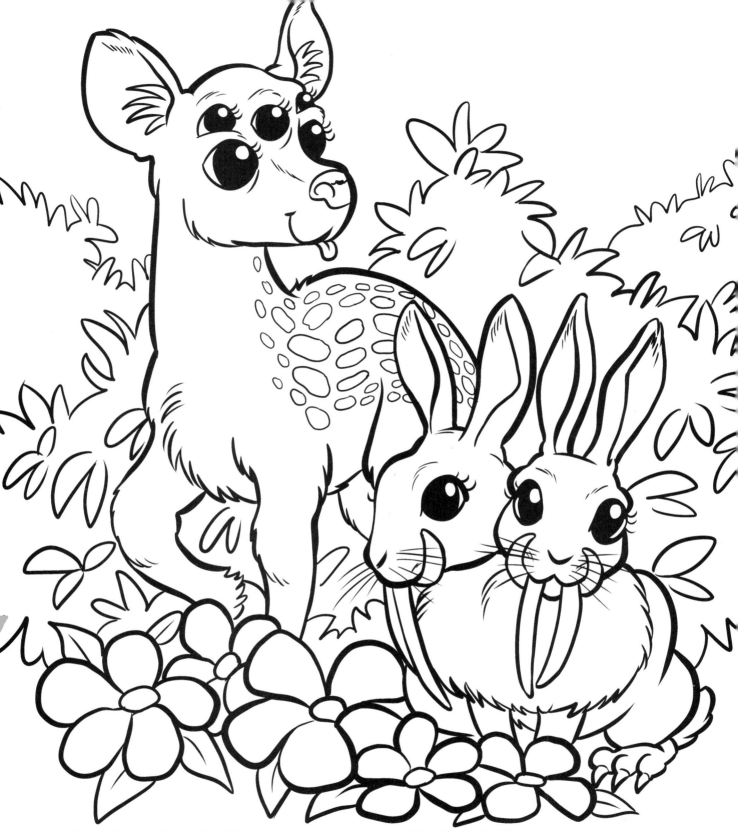

The local wildlife might be a little different after
the Earth becomes a nuclear wasteland.

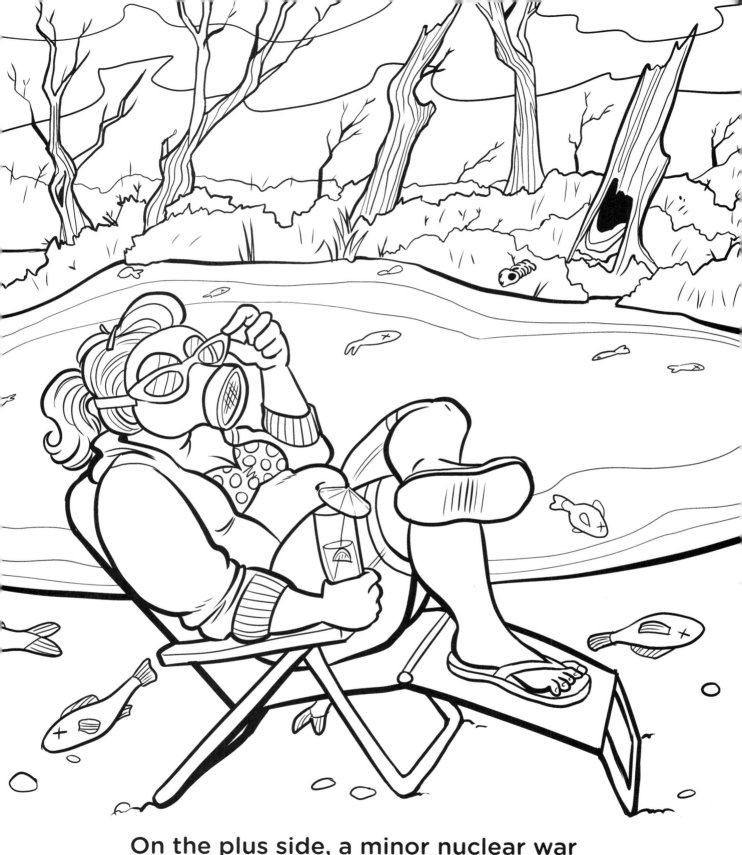

On the plus side, a minor nuclear war
will produce a nice, mild summer!

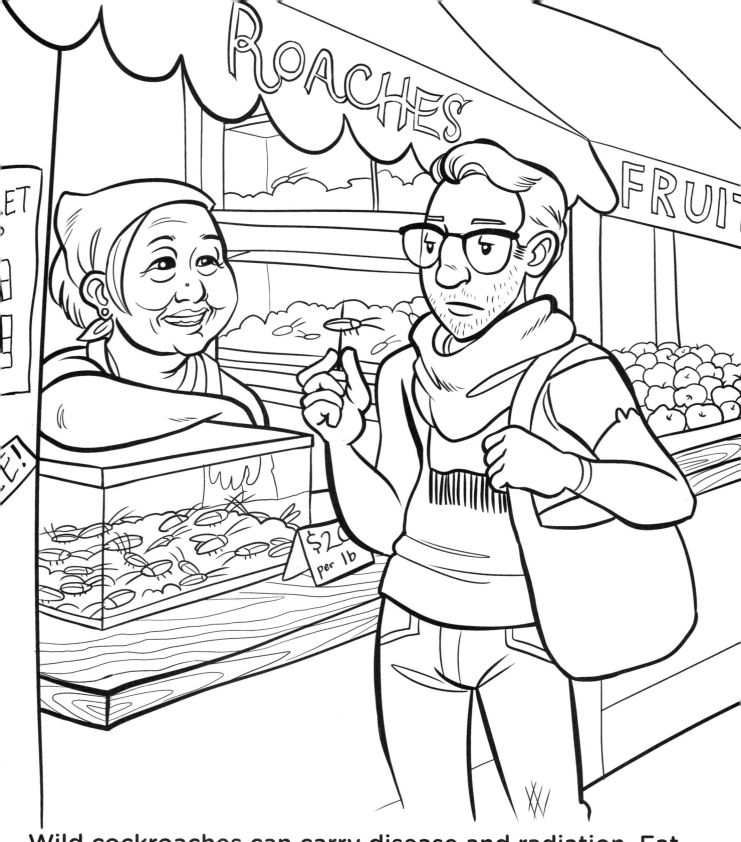

Wild cockroaches can carry disease and radiation. Eat organic, ethically-sourced cockroaches, not free-range.

Complete the crossword puzzle to reveal the contents of Jimmy's survival pantry!

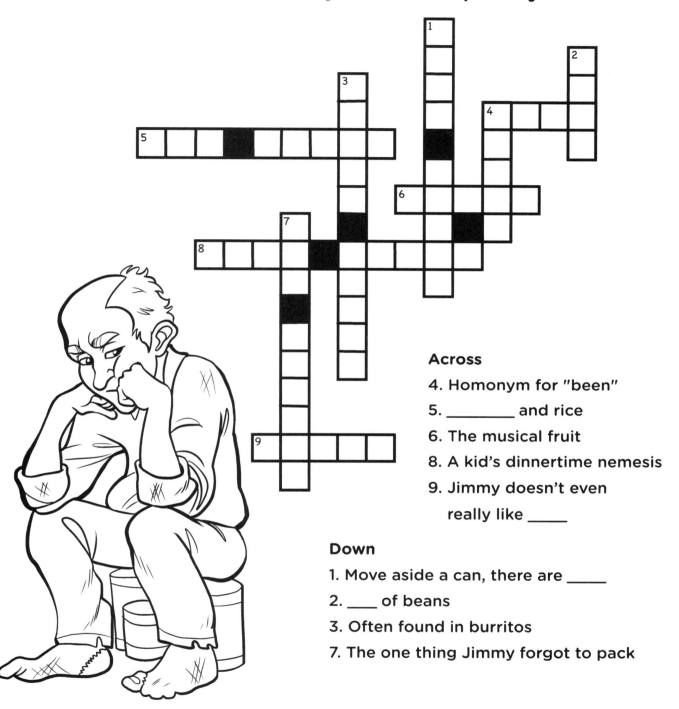

Across

4. Homonym for "been"

5. _____ and rice

6. The musical fruit

8. A kid's dinnertime nemesis

9. Jimmy doesn't even

    really like _____

Down

1. Move aside a can, there are _____

2. ____ of beans

3. Often found in burritos

7. The one thing Jimmy forgot to pack

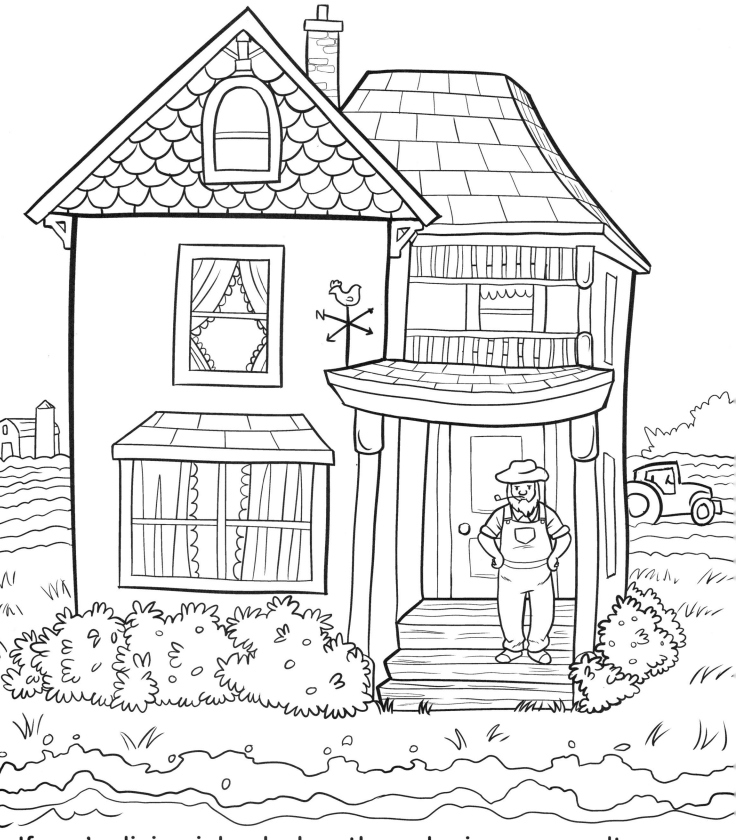

If you're living inland when the polar ice caps melt, you might find you've suddenly got oceanfront property!

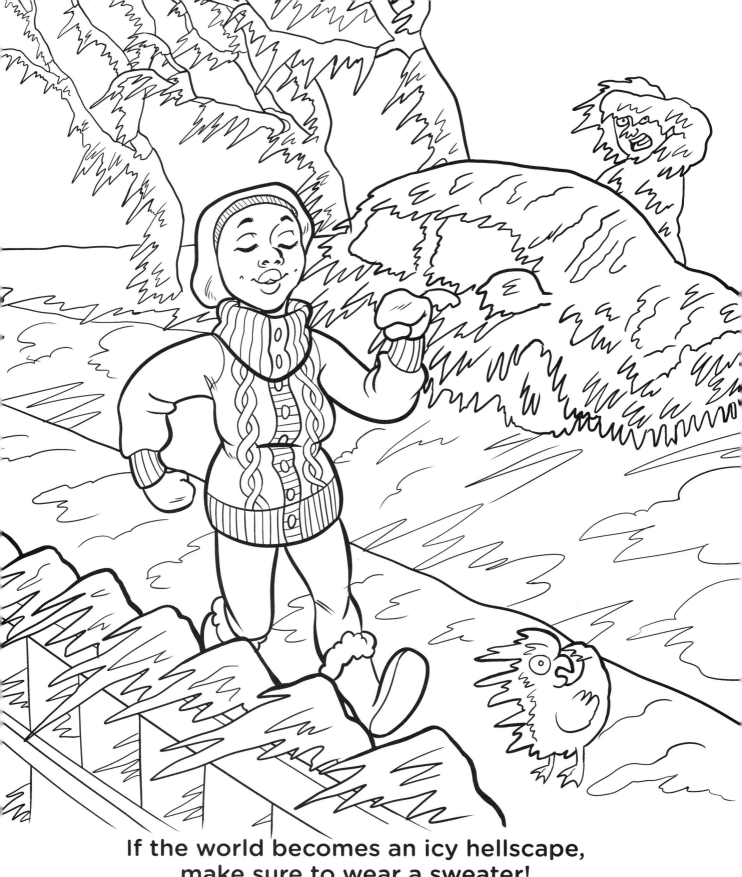

If the world becomes an icy hellscape,
make sure to wear a sweater!

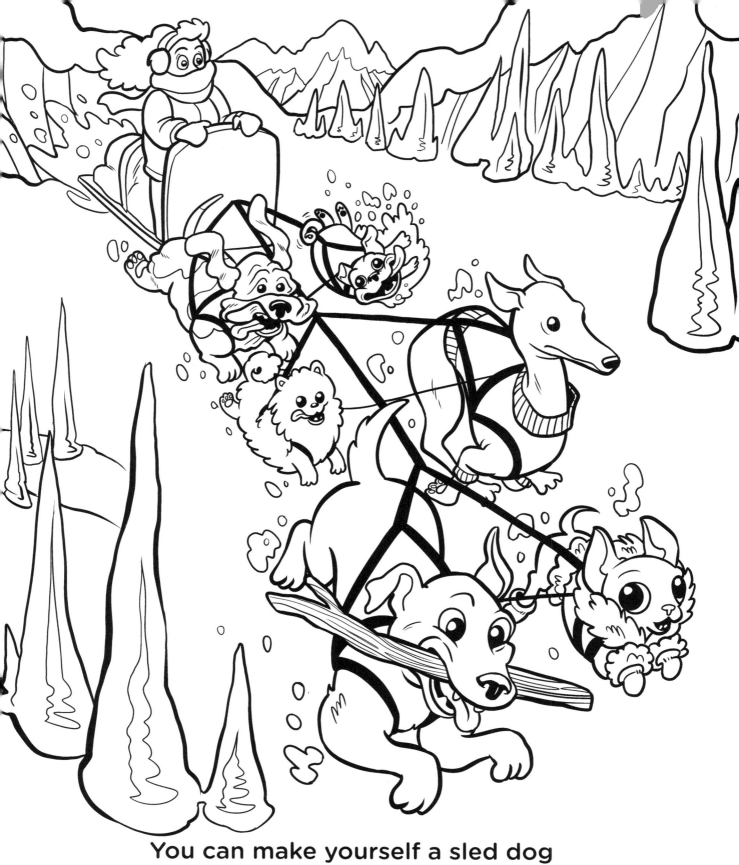

You can make yourself a sled dog
team from the local pound!

Color in the shapes with the dots to reveal a hidden inspirational message!

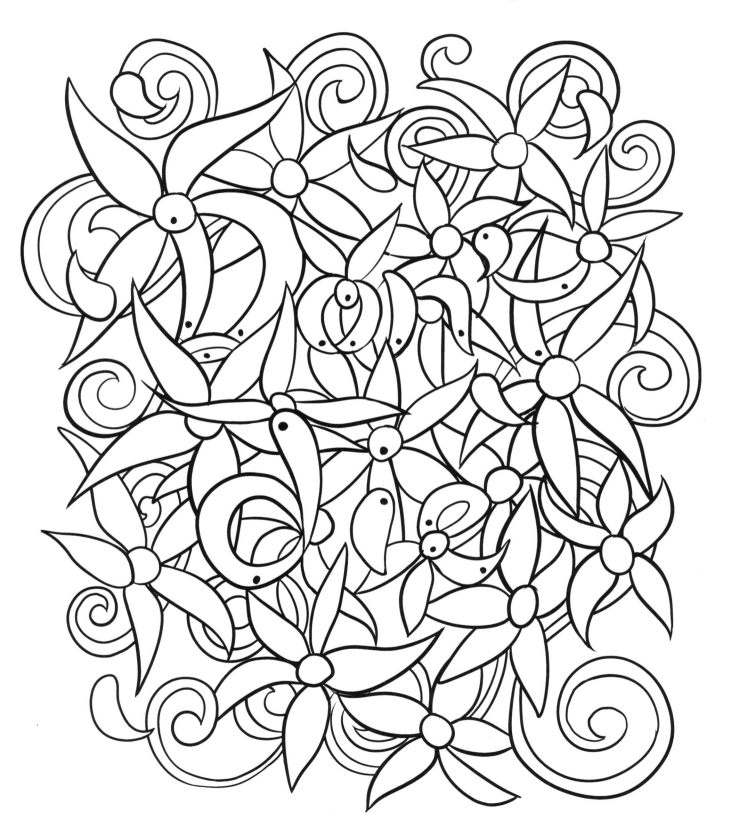

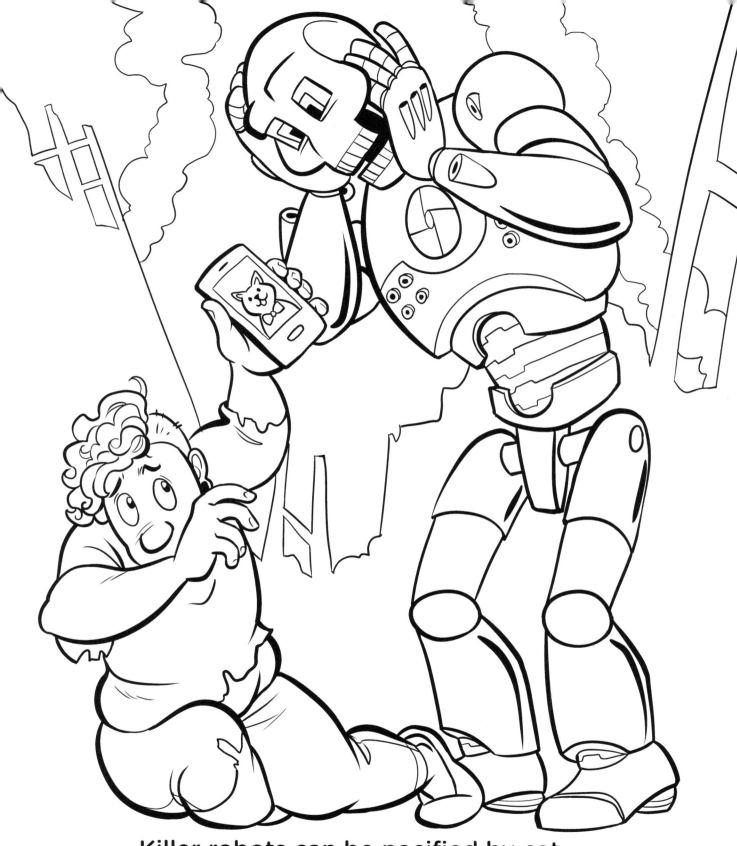

Killer robots can be pacified by cat
pictures. Stock up just in case.

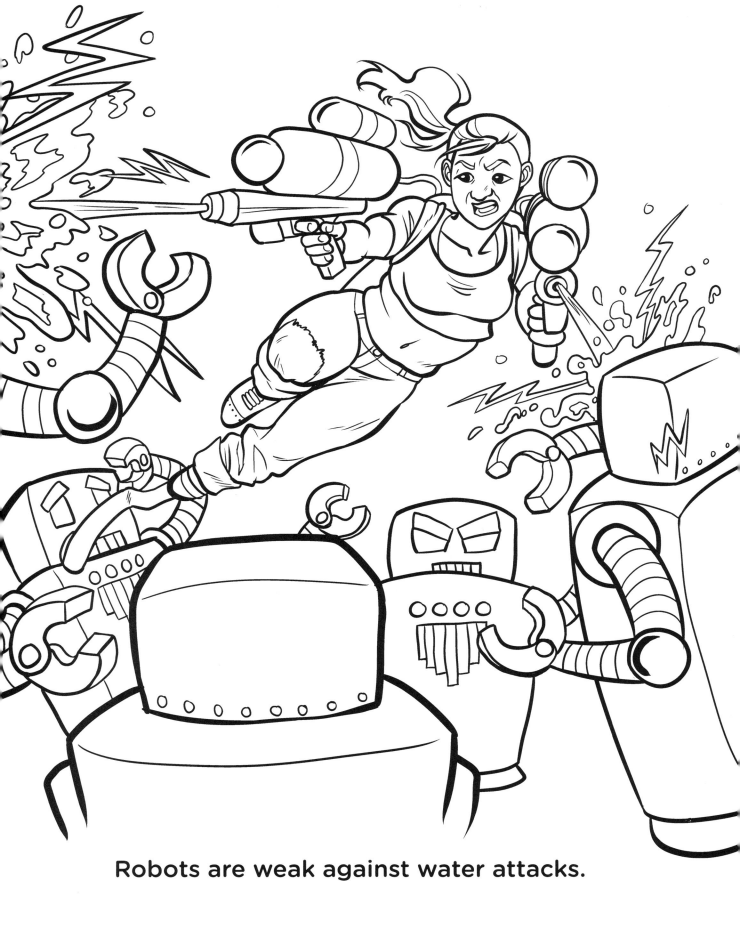

Robots are weak against water attacks.

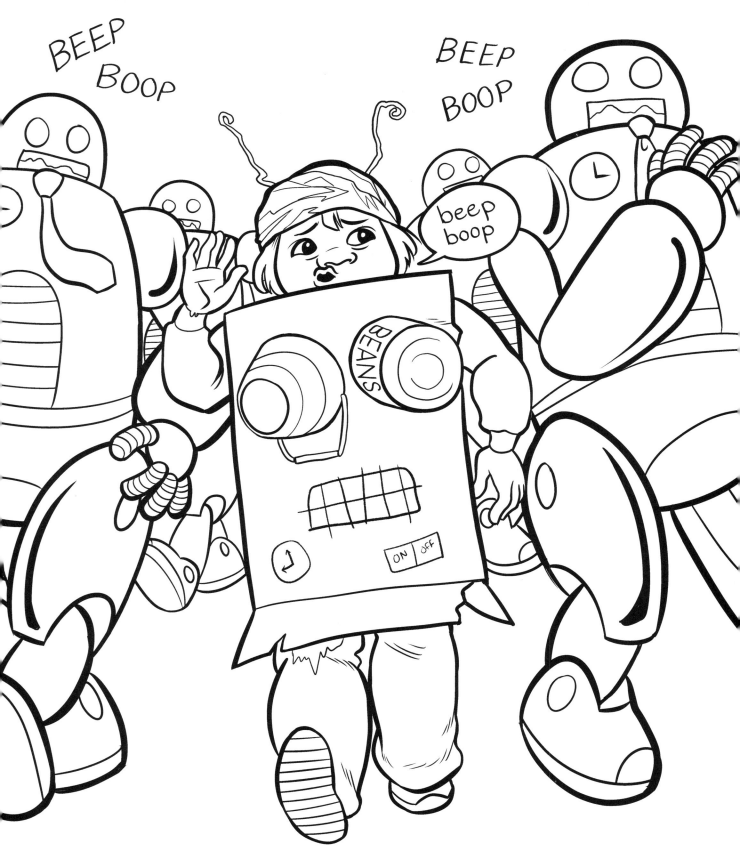

If you can't beat the robot overlords, join them.

Wondering if your ally is secretly a robot?
Take this quiz to find out!

1) What is your ally's best feature?

    a. Their unflinching way with a weapon

    b. Their open-mindedness

    c. Their beautiful monotone voice

2) When you find a fallen robot on the road, does your ally. . .

    a. Spit on its rusting husk

    b. Stand over it pensively, shaking their head

    c. Salute it discreetly and whisper, "Beep boop, comrade."

3) If you jump out and surprise them, does your ally. . .

    a. Pull out their weapon

    b. Throw their hands up and yell, "I have intel to trade!"

    c. Curse in binary

4) You are about to be surrounded by a group of killer robots. Does your ally. . .

    a. Look for a way to escape

    b. Attempt to reason with the killer robots

    c. Encourage your party to sit down
       and wait calmly for capture

5) When asked, "Are you a robot?"
   does your ally respond. . .

    a. "Uh, no."

    b. "So what if I was?"

    c. "I am not a robot, I love breathing.
       Oxygen is my fav L-O-L."

If you answered mostly a's, your ally is probably not a robot. If you answered mostly b's, your ally might not be a robot, but they might be a robot sympathizer; keep an eye on them! If you answered mostly c's, your ally is probably a robot.

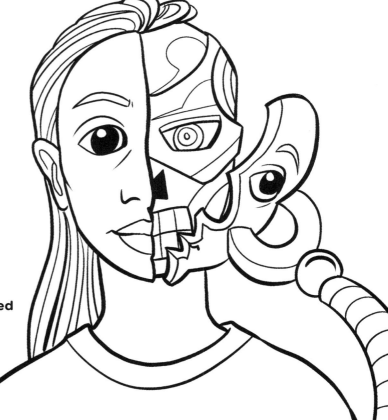

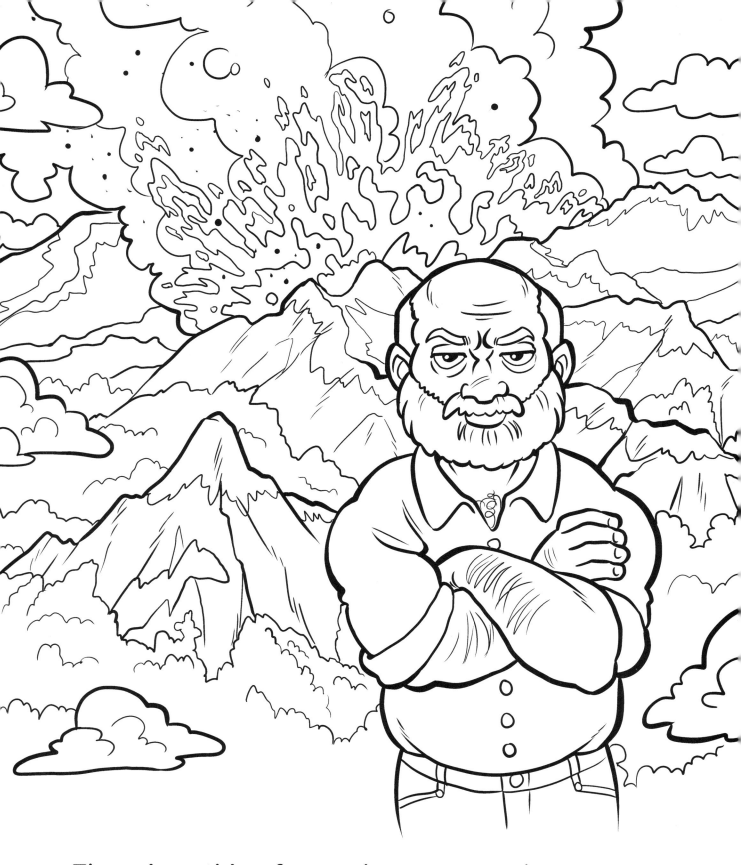

There is nothing funny about supervolcanoes.

Connect the dots to remind yourself what civilization used to be like before the world ended.

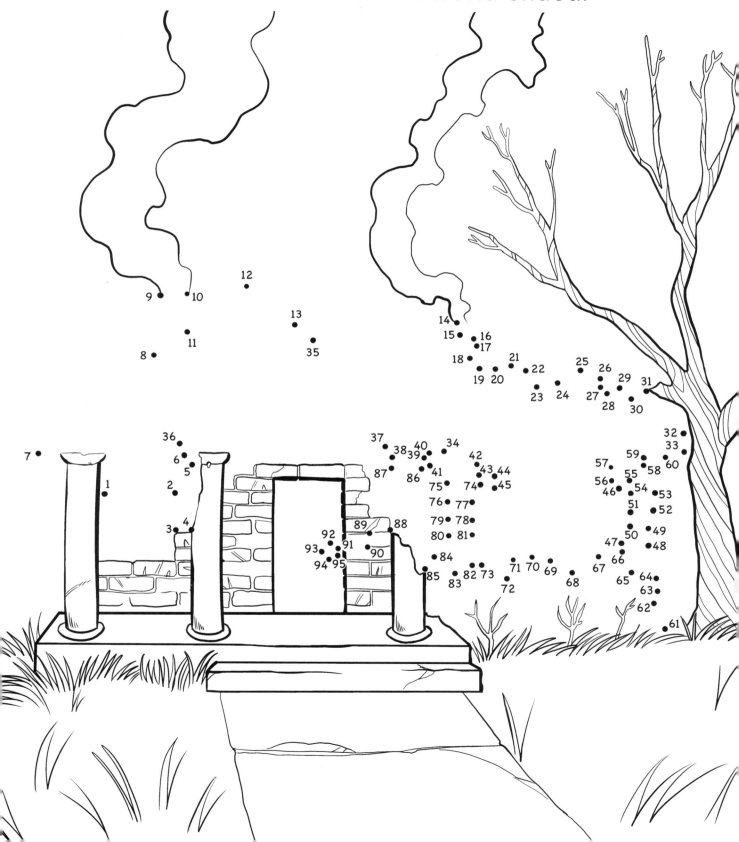

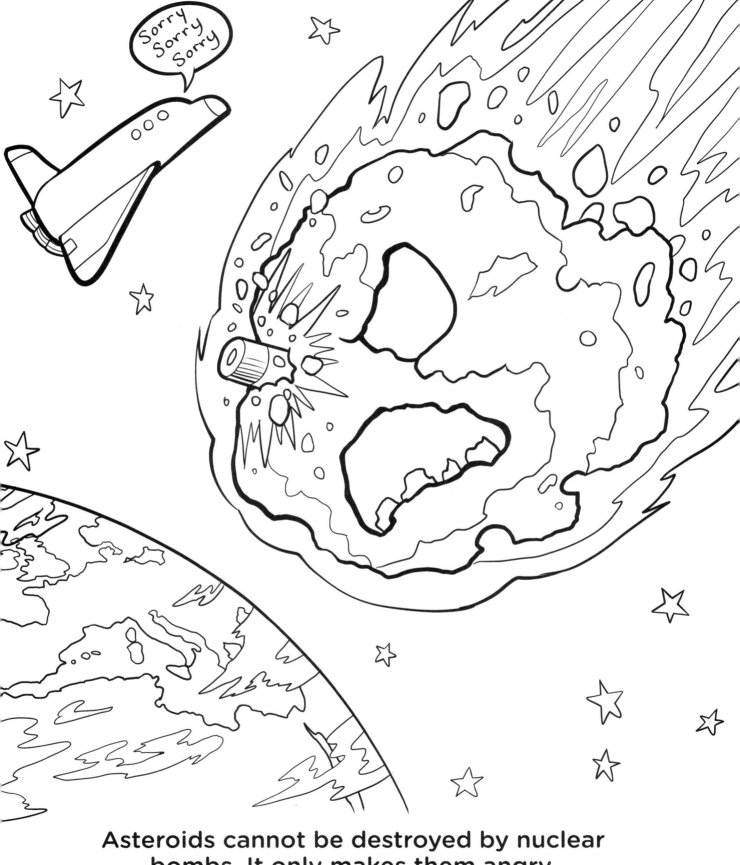

Asteroids cannot be destroyed by nuclear
bombs. It only makes them angry.

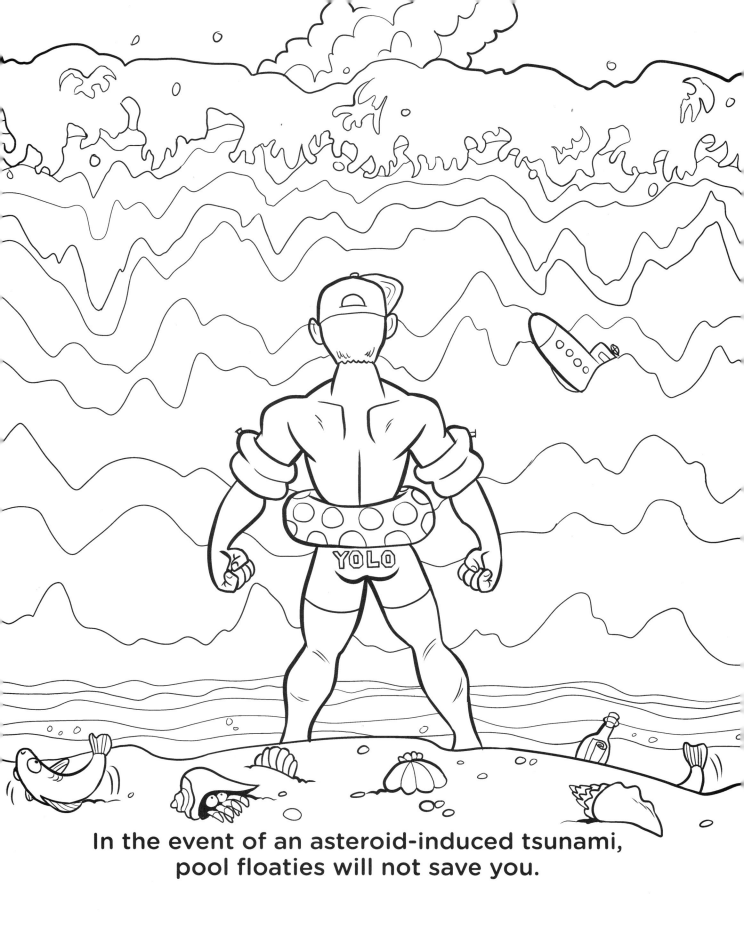

In the event of an asteroid-induced tsunami,
pool floaties will not save you.

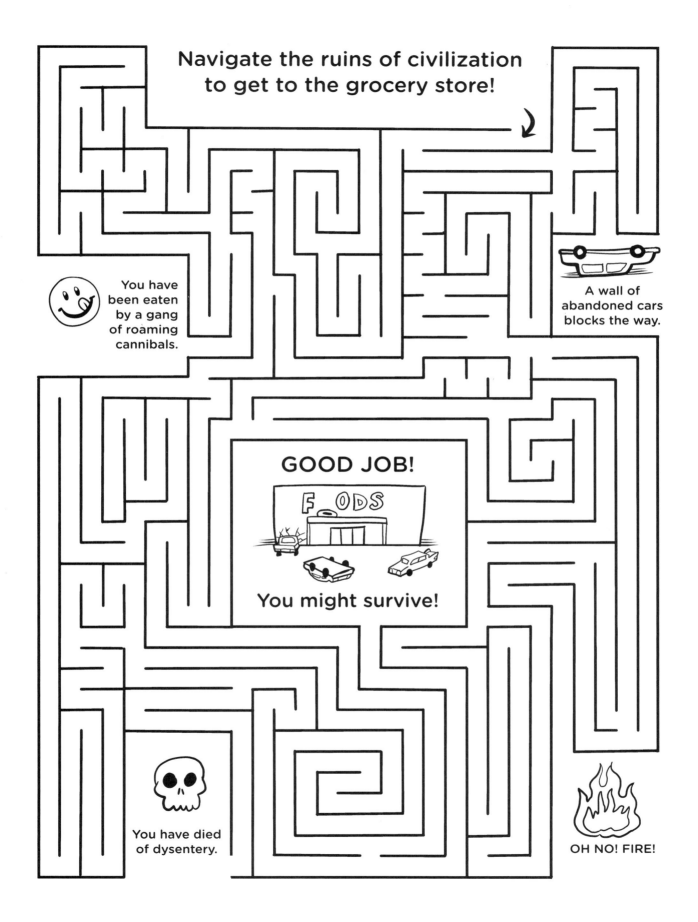

Navigate the ruins of civilization to get to the grocery store!

You have been eaten by a gang of roaming cannibals.

A wall of abandoned cars blocks the way.

GOOD JOB!

F_ODS

You might survive!

You have died of dysentery.

OH NO! FIRE!

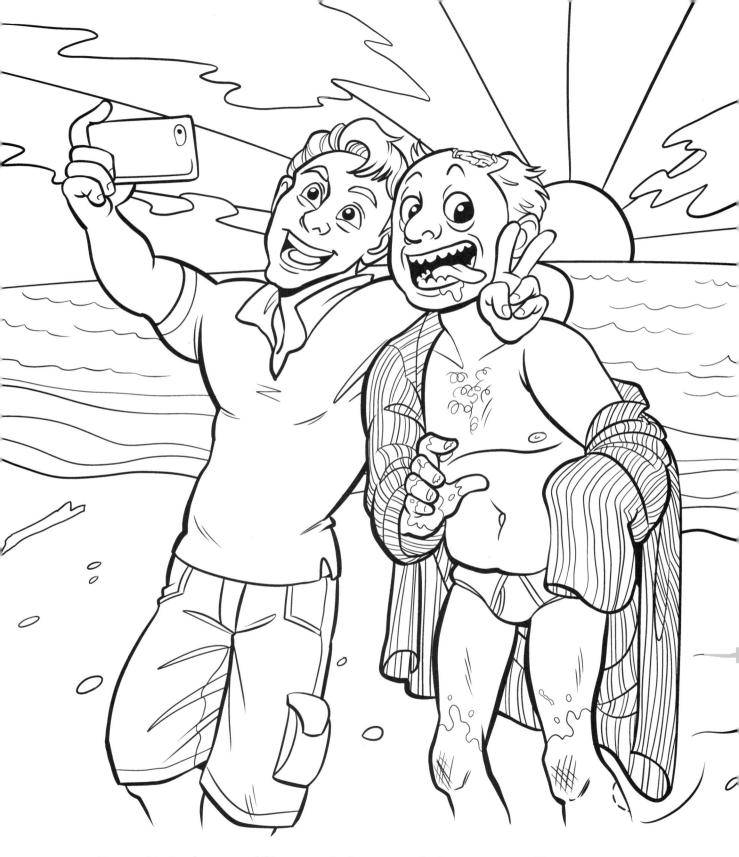

Don't take selfies with zombies. #nofingers

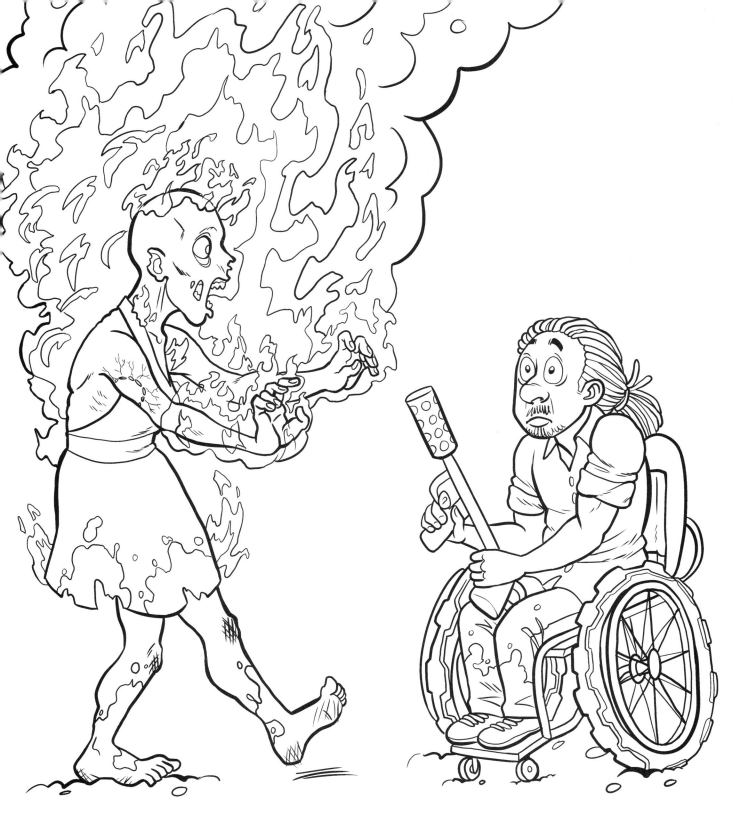

Tempting as it may be, do not set zombies on fire.
Fire just makes zombies ANGRY and ON FIRE.

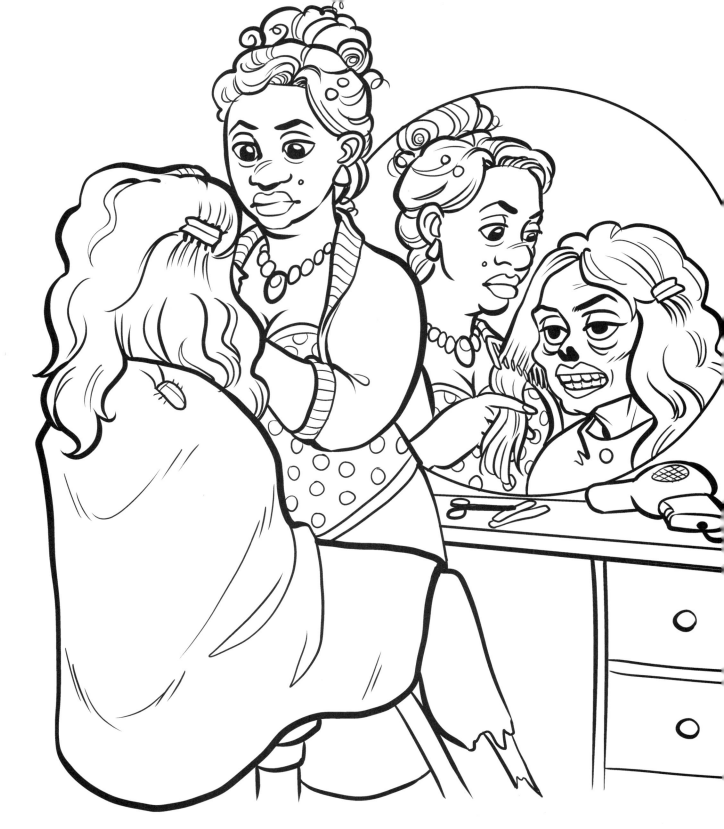

Work on building career skills that will be useful
in the eventual zombie-run global society.

Spot 5 differences between a survivor and a zombie!

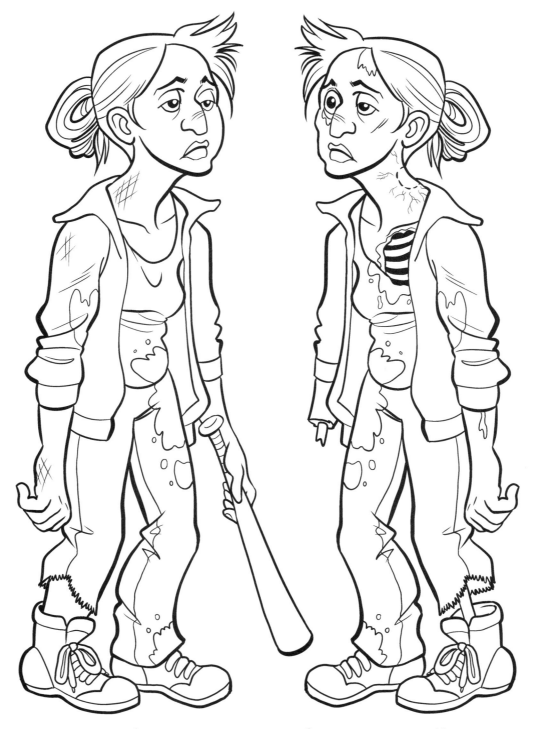

Answer Key: 1. The survivor is covered in zombie blood; the zombie is covered in human blood. 2. The survivor is slouching from exhaustion; the zombie is slouching from decomposition. 3. The survivor is thinking longingly of the Internet; the zombie thinks only of delicious flesh. 4. The survivor is filthy; the zombie is oozy. 5. The survivor is armed; the zombie is unarmed.

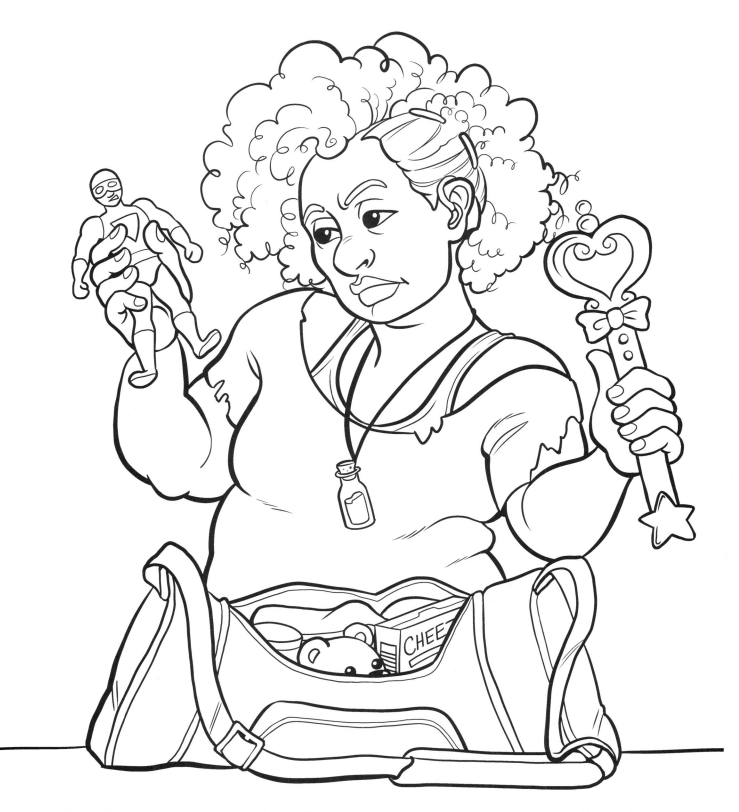

Pack a go-bag of only your most vital supplies in case you need to leave your stronghold quickly.

Match the alien species to the method of global domination!

1) Stealing Earth's water supply

2) Total nuclear annihilation

3) Enslaving humanity

4) They just want to be our friends!

5) Killing all humans with their own bare appendages

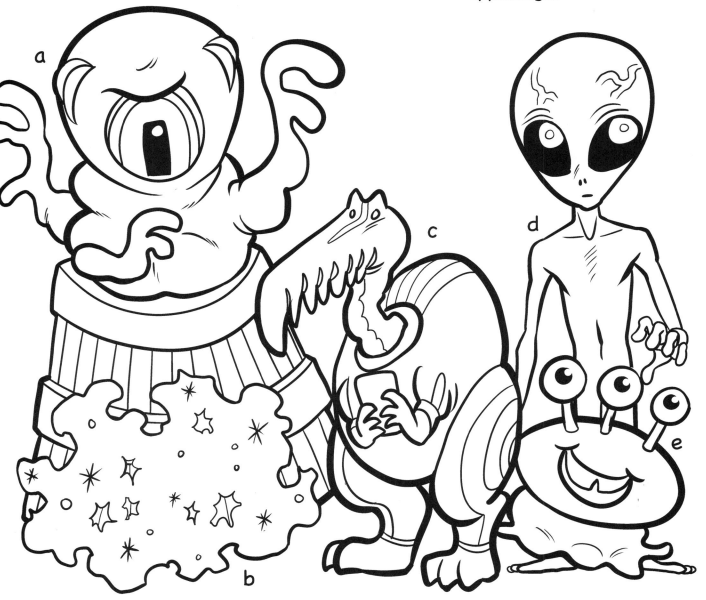

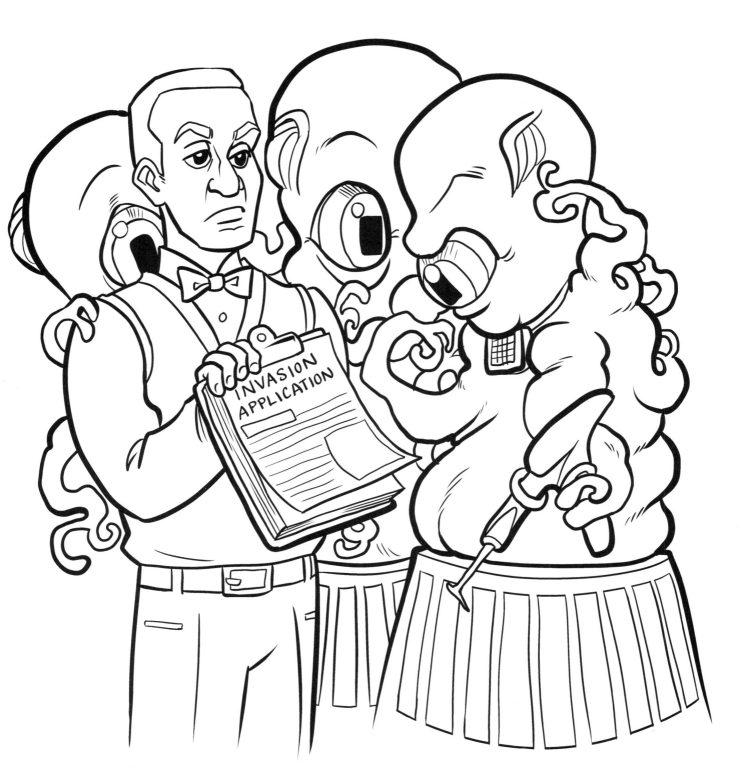

Bureaucracy is the most destructive force in the universe. Weaponize it if possible.

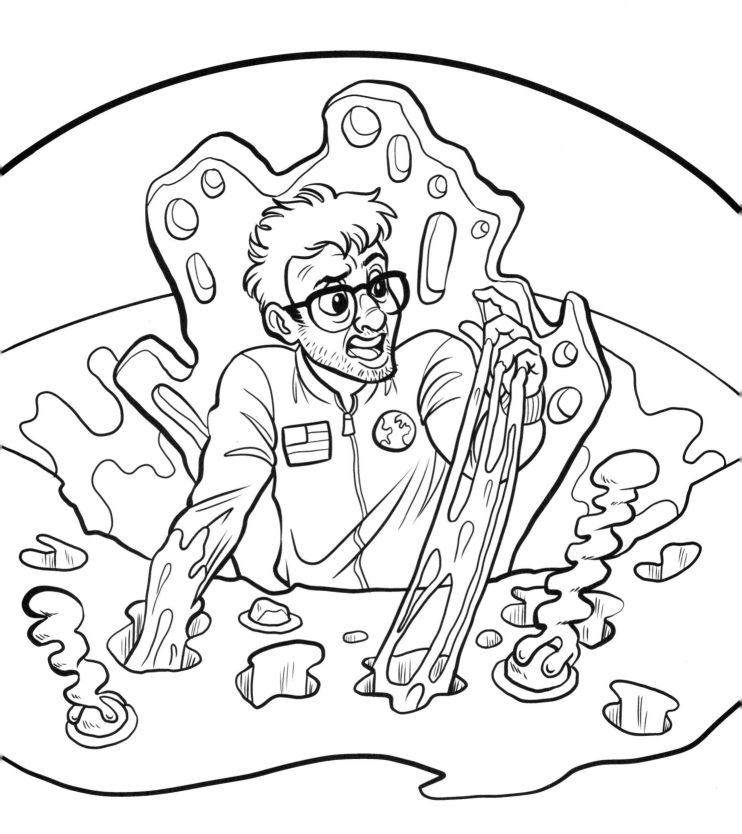

Alien spacecrafts are actually extremely
difficult for humans to fly.

Find these items from your bunker!

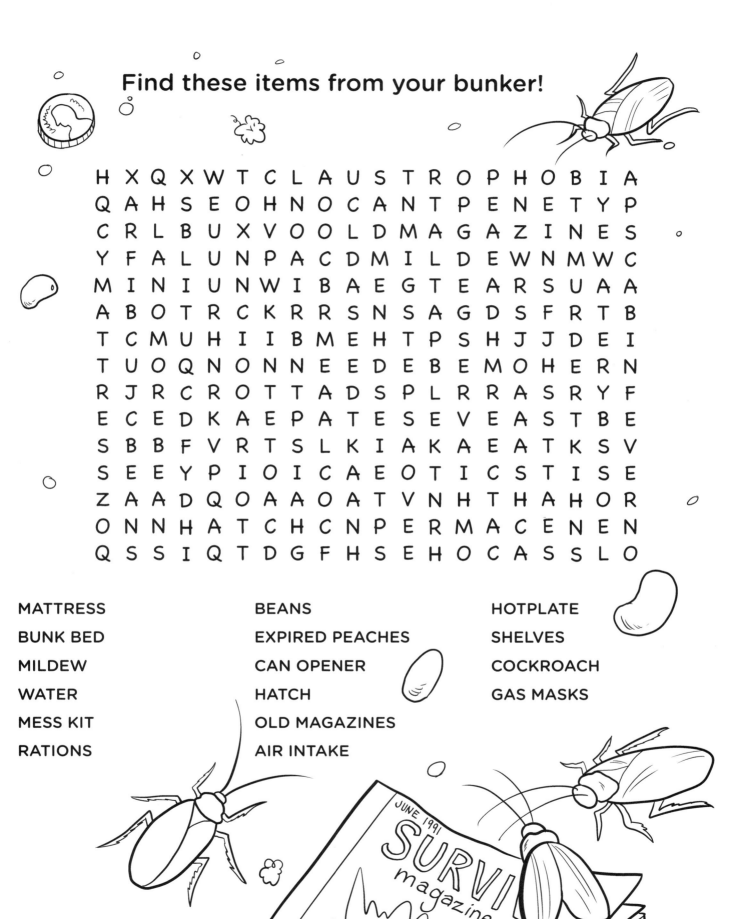

```
H X Q X W T C L A U S T R O P H O B I A
Q A H S E O H N O C A N T P E N E T Y P
C R L B U X V O O L D M A G A Z I N E S
Y F A L U N P A C D M I L D E W N M W C
M I N I U N W I B A E G T E A R S U A A
A B O T R C K R R S N S A G D S F R T B
T C M U H I I B M E H T P S H J J D E I
T U O Q N O N N E E D E B E M O H E R N
R J R C R O T T A D S P L R R A S R Y F
E C E D K A E P A T E S E V E A S T B E
S B B F V R T S L K I A K A E A T K S V
S E E Y P I O I C A E O T I C S T I S E
Z A A D Q O A A O A T V N H T H A H O R
O N N H A T C H C N P E R M A C E N E N
Q S S I Q T D G F H S E H O C A S S L O
```

MATTRESS

BUNK BED

MILDEW

WATER

MESS KIT

RATIONS

BEANS

EXPIRED PEACHES

CAN OPENER

HATCH

OLD MAGAZINES

AIR INTAKE

HOTPLATE

SHELVES

COCKROACH

GAS MASKS

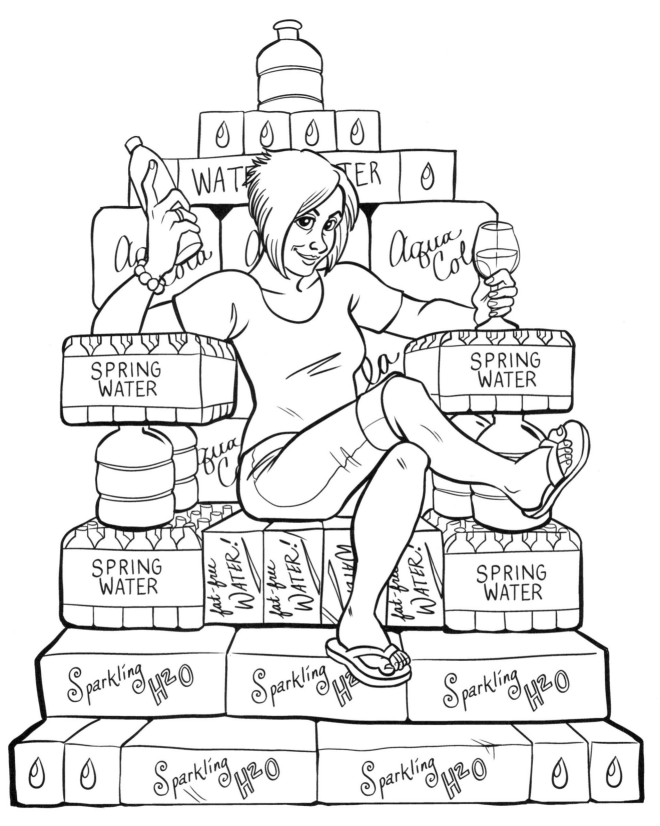

In a world where water is a precious commodity,
she who has the water makes the rules.

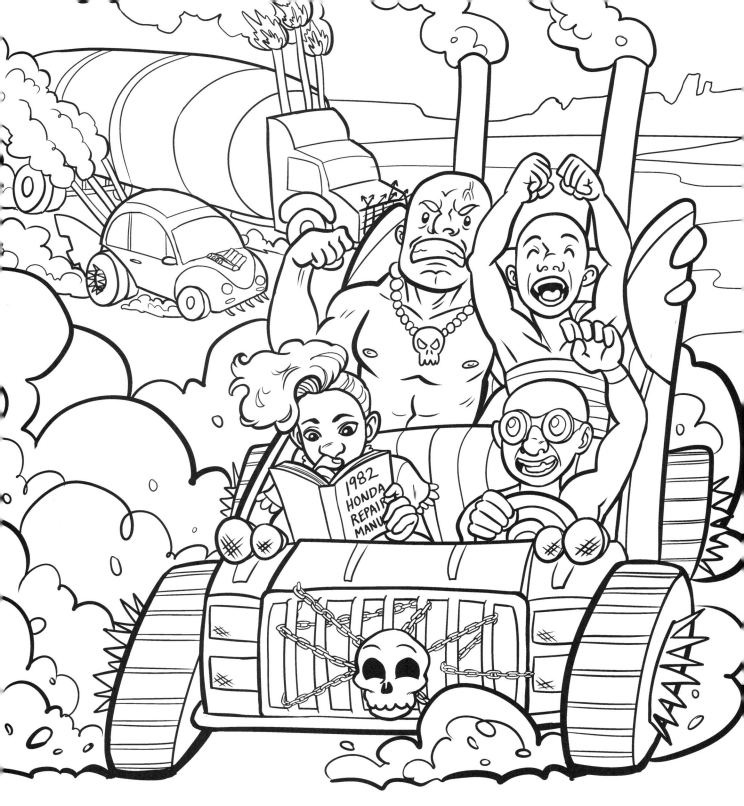

Brush up on auto maintenance in case the
post-apocalyptic wasteland is overrun
by engine-worshipping gangs.

Finish the drawing to design the vehicle you'll drive across the post-apocalyptic wasteland!

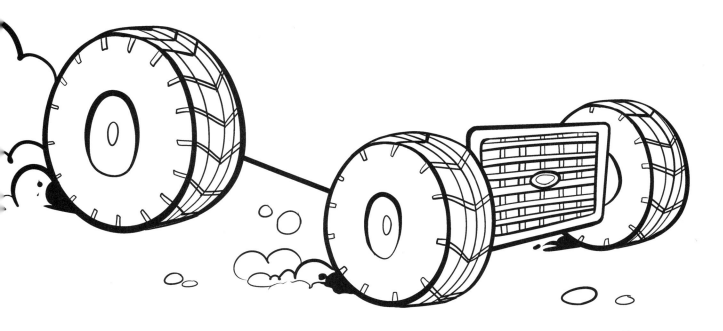

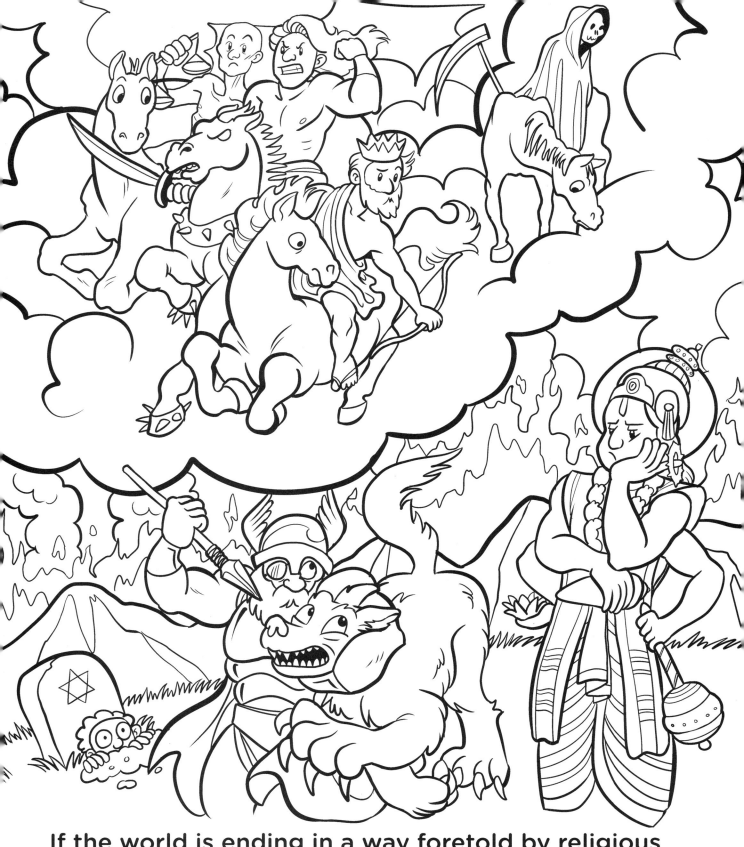

If the world is ending in a way foretold by religious texts, you are looking for advice in the wrong book.

Fill in the blanks to invent a new religious apocalypse!

When the chosen _____ have returned to _____
                  group of people   place

and _____ has risen to power, a _____ force
        proper noun   adjective

will appear. All the _____ will wither in the fields.
                        plural noun

A mighty _____ will sound. The _____ will tear
              noise   noun

asunder, and from _____ will come _____ fearsome
                      place   number

_____, bearing _____ _____. They will
  plural noun   adjective   plural noun

_____ the Earth, causing all of humanity to suffer
  verb

_____, until the believers are taken to _____.
unpleasant noun   place

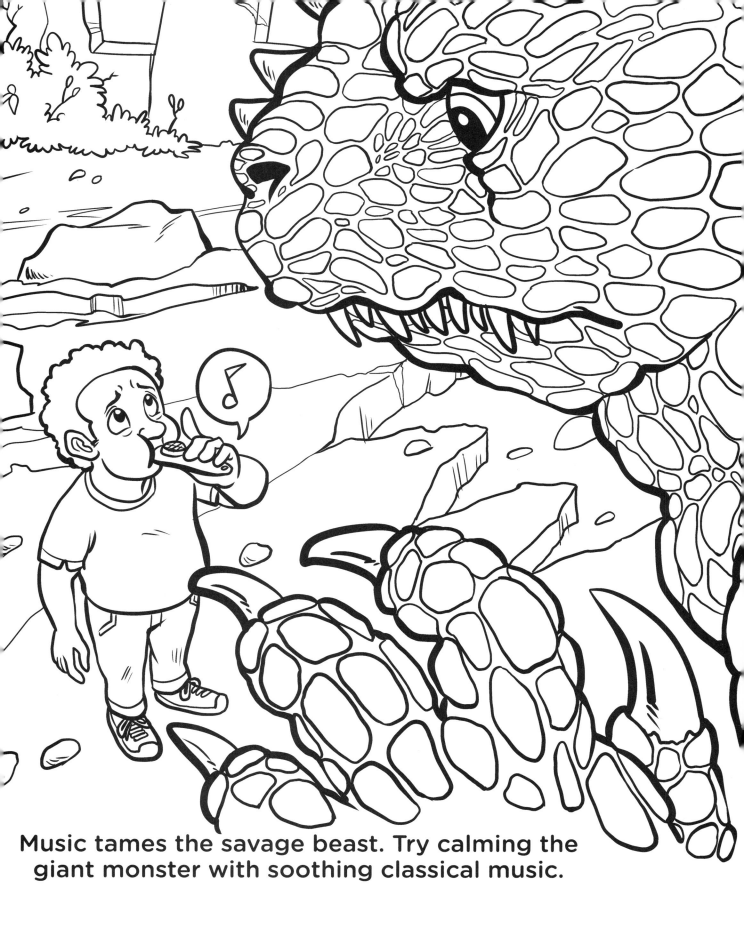

Music tames the savage beast. Try calming the giant monster with soothing classical music.

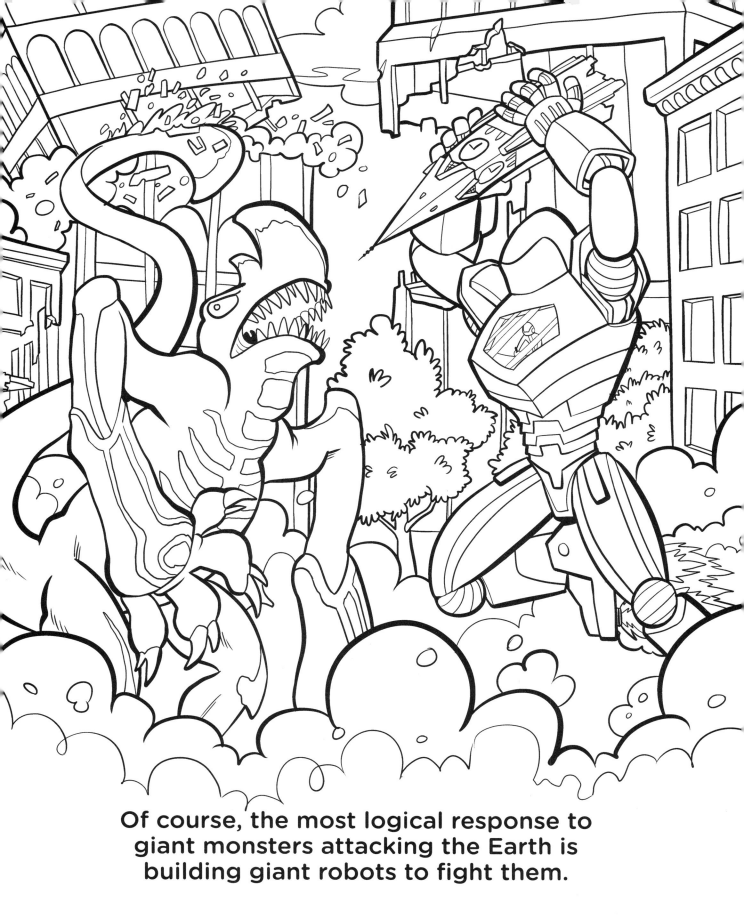

Of course, the most logical response to giant monsters attacking the Earth is building giant robots to fight them.

Cut out and dress up your very own monster-fighting giant robot paper doll!

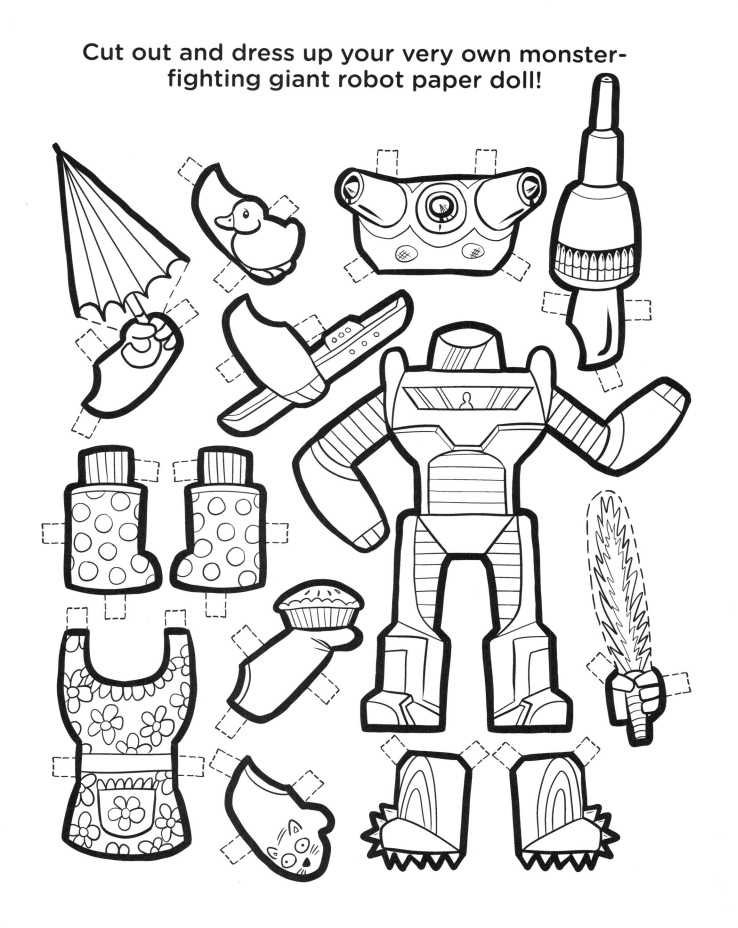

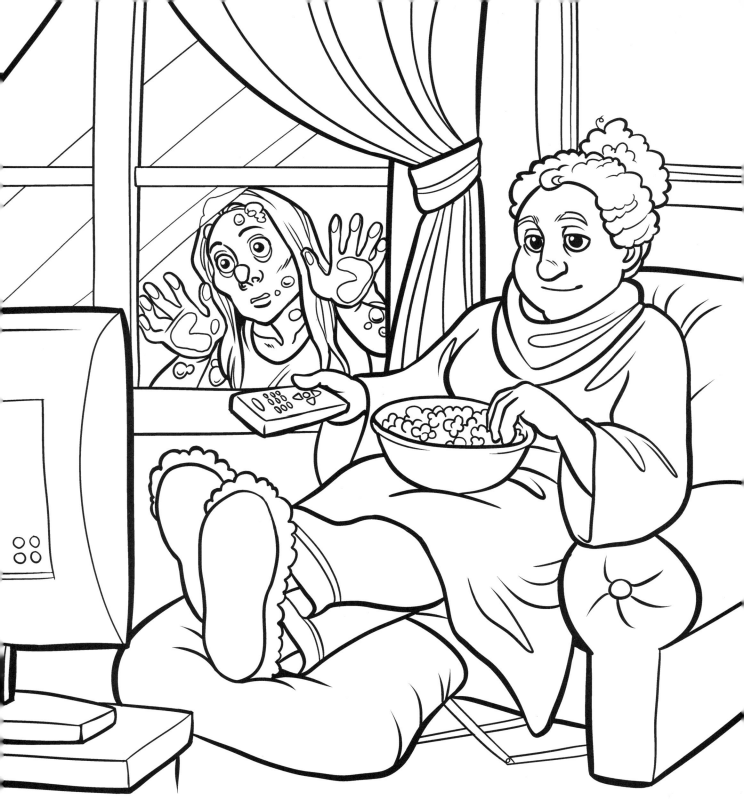

If a plague is wiping out the rest of humanity,
don't be a hero. Stay at home
and watch all ten seasons of *Friends*.

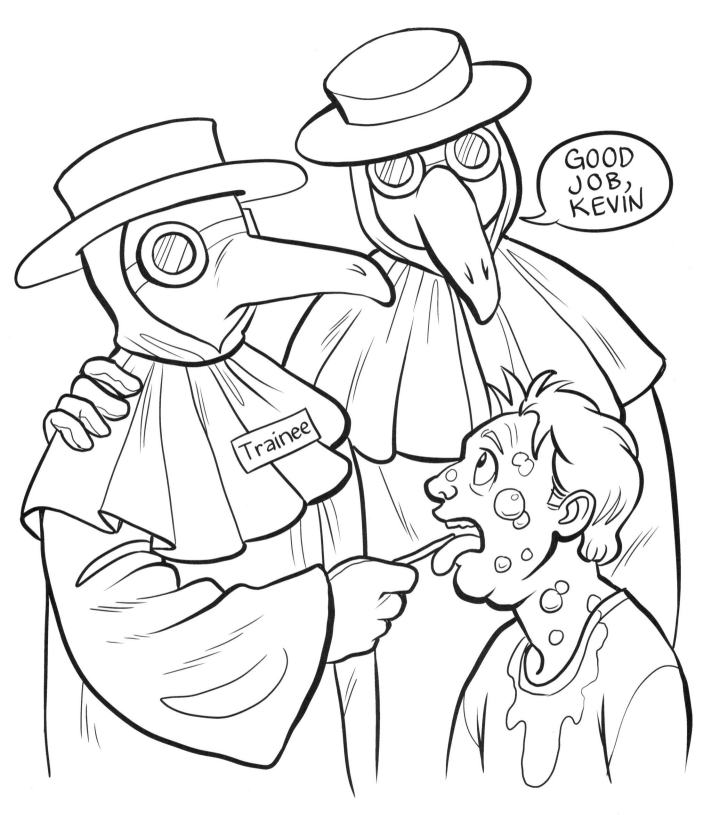

The apocalypse is a perfect time to
try your hand at a new career!

Draw your own imaginary bunker friend!

My friend _____

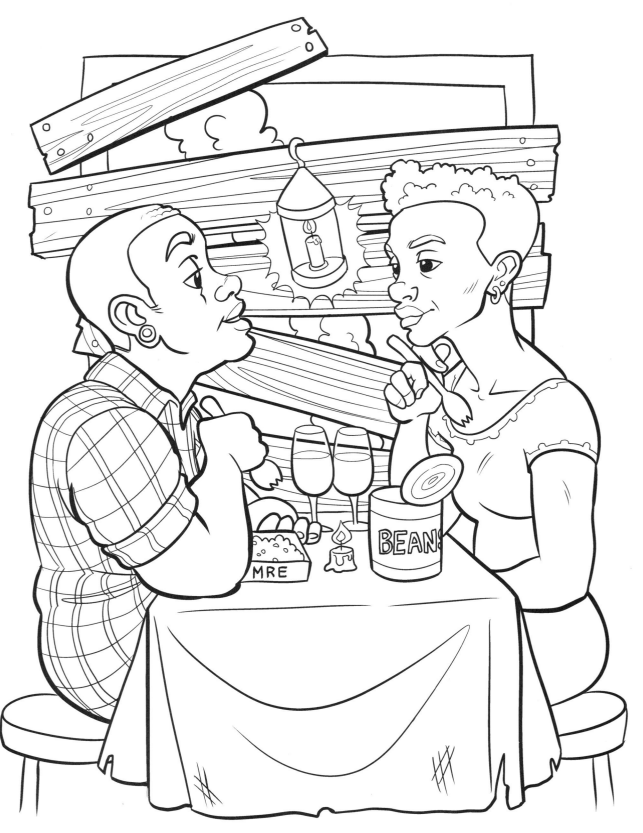

If an electromagnetic pulse wipes out all electricity,
it's a good time to have a romantic dinner for two.

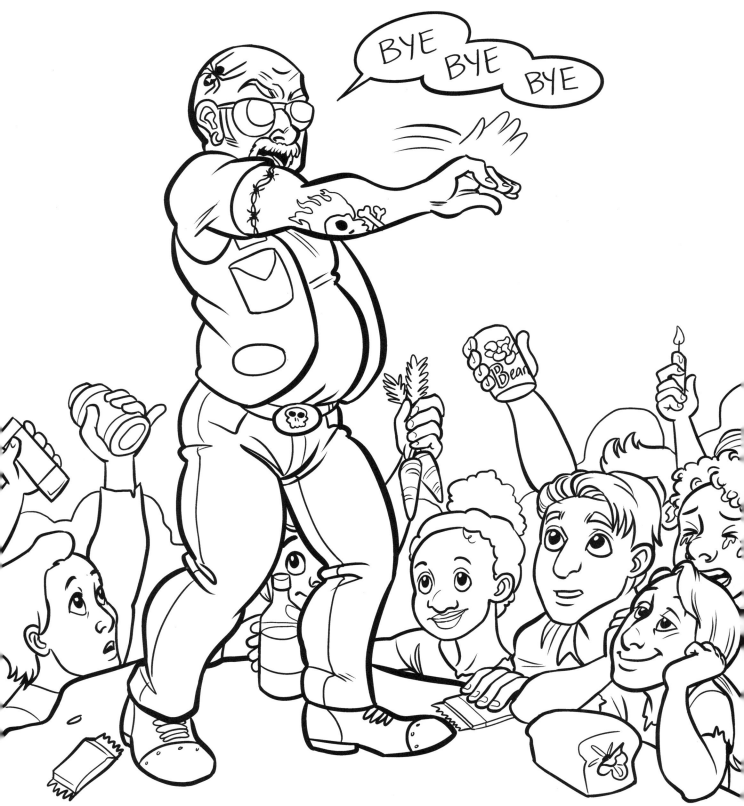

In the time after music players, your encyclopedic knowledge of boy band song and dance routines will finally be appreciated.

Describe or draw a meme you want to preserve after the internet is a distant memory!

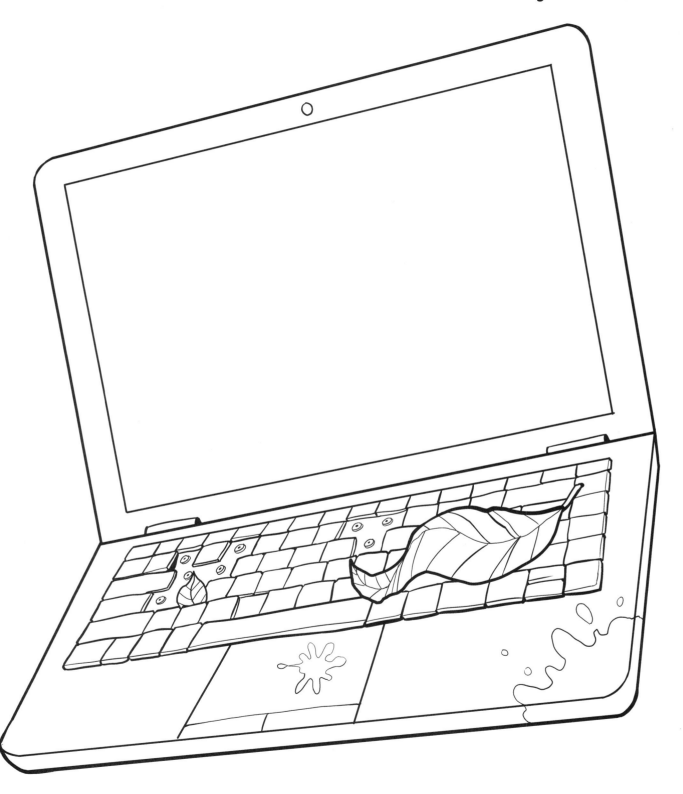

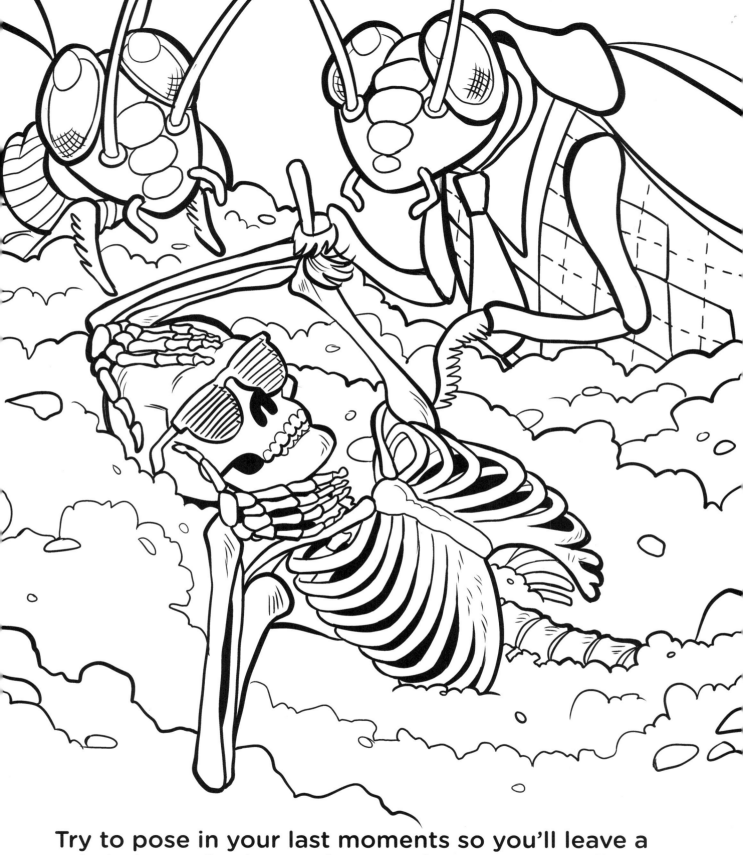

Try to pose in your last moments so you'll leave a cool skeleton for humanity's replacements to dig up.

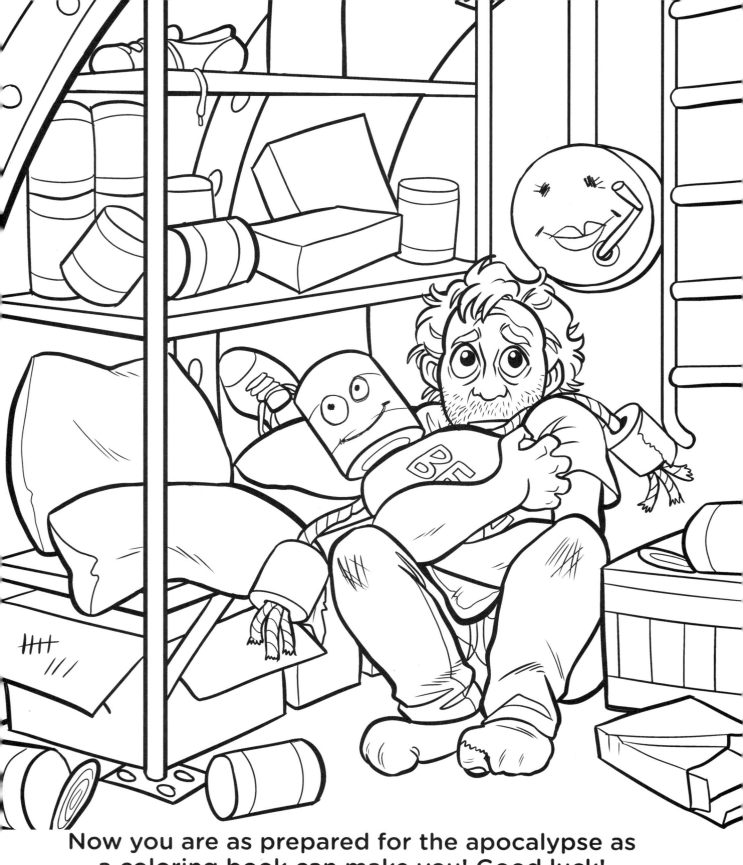

Now you are as prepared for the apocalypse as
a coloring book can make you! Good luck!